9 There was once a National "Serve Vegetables in Jell-O Week." Recommendations included radishes and cucumber in lime Jell-O and carrots and cabbage in lemon.

10 In 1993 in Batavia, New York, some curious medical folks hooked an EEG (electroencephalograph) up to Jell-O and found the wavelengths imitate those of the human brain.

11 You'll find a note on the side of Jell-O boxes about what not to add. An enzyme called bromelain found in fresh or frozen pineapple prevents Jell-O from solidifying. Besides pineapple, stay away from kiwi, ginger root, papaya, figs, and guava.

12 The Gowanus Studio Space in Brooklyn, New York, holds an annual Jell-O Mold Competition. The 2010 winner's piece was entitled "Aspic Ascension—Tastes Like Heaven" and featured molds of the Virgin Mary made of Bloody Mary Jell-O.

13 There is a Jell-O Gallery in Le Roy, New York, the birthplace of the confection. It's open year-round.

Jiggle Shots

75 RECIPES
To Get the PARTY Started

Rachel Federman

Abrams Image, New York

Editor: Lindley Boegehold
Designer: Laura Crescenti
Cover Photo: Elise Sheppard
Photographer: Carrie Jordan
Production Manager: Alison Gervais

Library of Congress Cataloging-in-Publication Data

Federman, Rachel.
Jiggle shots : 75 recipes to get the party started /
Rachel Federman.
        p. cm.
Includes bibliographical references and index.
ISBN 978-0-8109-9885-8 (alk. paper)
1. Gelatin shots. 2. Cocktails. I. Title.
TX814.5.G4F43 2011
641.8'642--dc22

                    2010044000

ISBN 978-0-8109-9885-8

The author and Harry N. Abrams, Inc. urge readers
to use their discretion and good sense in making
these jello shots and not do anything that seems
ill-advised. Finally, responsible drinking is everyone's
personal responsibility.

Printed and bound in U.S.A.

10 9 8 7 6 5 4 3 2 1

Abrams Image books are available at special
discounts when purchased in quantity for
premiums and promotions as well as fundraising
or educational use. Special editions can also be
created to specification. For details, contact
specialmarkets@abramsbooks.com or the
address below.

ABRAMS
THE ART OF BOOKS SINCE 1949

115 West 18th Street
New York, NY 10011
www.abramsbooks.com

Introduction

What can simultaneously conjure up the innocence of summer days in suburbia—where kids with names like Mary and Timmy come running across the lawn for an afternoon snack—and a bunch of sweaty college kids cramming into dorm rooms, licking body shots off one another's stomachs?

Jell-O shots! They're whimsical, bright, colorful, and slightly deviant. They put the "jiggle" into giggle juice, the punch into indulgence, the flavor into firewater. Their unreal neon flavors will stain your lips and make you forget that you are drinking a lot more than the Kool-Aid. . . . And these vibrant treats are a rite of passage. "Have you done Jell-O shots?" you may hear partygoers ask each other on that most eagerly anticipated of young adult birthdays.

What does doing shots entail exactly?
Whatever you want it to. Pop them into your mouth, "inject" them, make temporary body art, experiment with different colors and layers. Pick your poison and your favorite Jell-O flavor and see how they taste together. Add whipped cream, fruit slices, or gumdrops. Make "zippers" for an outdoor party, for a new neighbor, for a girls' night in, or guys' night out. Try team colors for sports events. Concoct seasonal varieties for holidays. You can make an old-fashioned Jell-O mold for everyone to share, cut Jell-O into squares, sculpt with cookie cutters, or use plain old ice cube trays.

While you're mixing, pouring, and waiting for shots to set, you'll be in good company. Long a Friday-night staple for the down-and-dirty college set, Jell-O shots have now established themselves as a legitimate cocktail. When Orthodox Jews serve Manischewitz shots at a Passover Seder, kids in Texas are suspended for selling Jell-O shots at school, and karaoke bars in Kabukicho, Tokyo, are lined with gelatin tequila balls, you can be sure the wiggly snacks have hit the big time.

Today's creations are just the latest in a history of invention that began when Pearle B. Wait transformed gelatin dessert by adding a fruit flavor in 1897. It was his wife who came up with the name and the world said "hello" to Jell-O for the first time. In the 1950s, raspberry floating islands, orange parfait pies, and bowls of tapioca took over the kitchen landscape with a decidedly space-age feel. At a time when dessert was practically a recommended food group, moms likely had no idea just how much fun their grandchildren would one day have with this perennially popular dessert.

Ready to get started? All you need is a few boxes of Jell-O powder, boiling water, and your favorite moonshine. Later, when the lights are low and the music high, there'll be no need for guests to hover around the mixing table spilling ungodly amounts of high-end vodka. Want margaritas? Try lime and tequila dipped in salt. Something that doubles as dessert? Mix chocolate pudding with Baileys Irish Cream. A touch of sophistication? How about champagne glasses? Something to mark the beginning of summer vacation? Make portable little Mojitos with fresh mint.

They're fun to prepare and they sure go down easy. Try new flavors. Try new colors. Express yourself. Go wild. Be a kid again (except for the 80-proof beverage part, of course). Nothing says "instant party" like a tray full of wiggly multicolored little cocktails. Bottoms up. But not for long.

Getting Started...

For the most part, the making of spoonable cocktails is almost as easy as getting them down the hatch. For a basic Jell-O shot, you simply mix Jell-O powder with boiling liquid (usually water, but it can be juice or even champagne) in a heatproof bowl or pitcher and let it cool. Give it a little stir and then add the remaining liquids (these should be chilled): water, brandy, or lime juice, to name just a few. Let the concoction ever so slightly begin to thicken——especially if using paper cups——and pour into whatever shot glasses you are using. Small plastic cups work as well as paper, and condiment containers (with tops for easy transport) are a favorite. You can also use real shot glasses, champagne glasses, or even paper cupcake wrappers. Certain containers lend themselves to squeezing out a shot in one piece, while real glass often requires a spoon to dig and poke about. Some people recommend spraying cups with PAM beforehand, while others suggest running a toothpick along the edge between the Jell-O and the cup after each shot has set. Then again, there are those who prefer to give their tongues a workout. Chances are, your guests won't be picky as to how they get the jiggly stuff into their mouths, but they're sure to appreciate an artistic arrangement. Also, it helps to pour the mixture from the bowl to a little pitcher before pouring it into individual cups. Make sure to allow at least four hours for shots to solidify.

Pudding shots are even easier; they don't require any boiling, cooling, or setting. (If friends are coming over in a half hour, pudding shots are the way to go.) Always choose the instant kind. Working with a blender or an electric mixer will get you a nice smooth texture. A whisk is the next best thing, but you can certainly make do with a fork and a little bit of stamina (and you might even like the chunky, not-quite-mixed-all-the-way cake batter effect).

Once pudding shots are set, they can be gobbled right up or kept in the fridge or freezer. Most pudding-shot recipes require Cool Whip, which should be taken out of the freezer and thawed first. This is the step that requires the most patience. Cool Whip is incredibly sticky and irritating when partially frozen. Anything less than a full thaw will result in several rounds of obscenities!

How many shots does a typical recipe make? The standard single package of Jell-O or pudding makes about 12 small (1-ounce) or 6 large (2-ounce) shots. The large are each roughly the equivalent of half an ordinary shot, which might make it sound like you are home free, but stop and ask yourself: When was the last time you pounded four shots before even trying the guacamole? (If the answer is last night, and you're reading this to prep for tonight, then your recovery time would put Usain Bolt to shame.)

Regardless, the shot size is up to you. They don't all have to match but remember they are supposed to be a mouthful. Then again, in form if not in function, the variations are infinite: you can serve the treats as little parfaits in ice-cream dishes, if you like. Or you can set out one big punch bowl, hand out spoons, and let everyone dig in. If you're throwing a party, you'll likely want to at least double most recipes given here.

Since pudding shots don't need to set, you can quickly assess whether a heavy hand with the Triple Sec meant they came out too watery. More often than not, you can fix this by simply adding more Cool Whip. Then again, you can also serve these treats old-school——shots that you actually drink, albeit a bit sweeter and thicker than most.

You may or may not remember from high school chemistry that alcohol evaporates when heated at a lower temperature than water. Make sure you add the alcohol after the initial mix of Jell-O powder and water has come to

room temperature. In this case, haste really does make waste. Don't wait too long, though, or you'll see the pudding or Jell-O start to solidify.

There actually is a science to all of this. In fact, here is what Margaret Gardel, Ph.D., assistant physics professor at the Institute for Biophysical Dynamics, University of Chicago, says about Jell-O solidification: "To keep its shape, the Jell-O needs to be primarily solid. As the alcohol content increases, the polymerization of the Jell-O is inhibited such that it becomes more fluid-like. At a critical threshold of alcohol, no solidification occurs. This transition can be measured with a rheometer."

In case you don't have a rheometer on hand, here are the important points to remember:

1 Stir Jell-O powder into boiling water in a heatproof bowl or pitcher

2 Allow to cool

3 Add the rest of the ingredients, as each recipe details

4 Into the fridge the shots or molds go for 4 hours

Red

Accomplice

3-ounce package strawberry Jell-O
1 cup champagne, brought just
to a boil
2 ounces chilled lemon juice
5 ½ ounces chilled vodka

Stir Jell-O into champagne until powder is completely dissolved. Allow to cool 20 minutes. Add lemon juice and vodka. Mix and pour into shot glasses. Place shots in fridge to set.

Bourbon Street

3-ounce package strawberry Jell-O
5 ounces boiling water
4 ounces cold water
3 ounces chilled grain alcohol

Stir Jell-O into boiling water until powder is completely dissolved. Allow to cool 20 minutes. Add cold water and grain alcohol. Mix and pour into shot glasses. Place shots in fridge to set.

They really do serve this drink on Bourbon Street down in New Awlins. Super easy, but be careful—grain alcohol is 95 percent alcohol.

Chocolate-Covered Cherries

3-ounce package cherry Jell-O
1 cup boiling water
1 ounce heavy cream
6 ounces chilled crème de cacao
maraschino cherries

Stir Jell-O into boiling water until powder is completely dissolved. Beat in heavy cream. Add crème de cacao and mix. Fill cups; the smaller you make these shots, the better. As the shots begin to thicken, add a maraschino cherry to each. The stem should stick out of the top. Place shots in fridge to set.

Serve these treats popped out of their cups, so guests can pick them up by their stems and drop them in their mouths. You may need to run a toothpick along the edge of each cup and pop out the shot. It may require some handiwork (crushing the cup a little) to get the shot out in one piece, but eventually you'll get it.

Cape Cod

3-ounce package cranberry Jell-O
½ cup water and ½ cup ginger ale, brought just to a boil
5 ounces vodka
3 ounces cold water
juice from a fresh lime

Stir Jell-O into boiling water and ginger ale mixture until powder is completely dissolved. Allow to cool 20 minutes. Add vodka, cold water, and lime juice and mix. Pour into shot glasses. Place shots in fridge to set.

Cosmic Cosmo

3-ounce package cranberry Jell-O
1 cup boiling water
3 ounces cold water
4 ounces chilled citron vodka
2 ounces chilled Cointreau

Stir Jell-O into boiling water until powder is completely dissolved. Allow to cool 20 minutes. Add cold water, vodka, and Cointreau. Mix and pour into shot glasses. Place shots in fridge to set.

For a Cosmo Royale, substitute:
cold Rose's Sweetened Lime
  Juice for cold water
plain vodka for citron vodka
1 ounce Cointreau, 1 ounce
  Chambord for 2 ounces
  Cointreau

Game Ball

3-ounce package cherry Jell-O
1 cup cola, brought just to a boil
6 ounces chilled white rum
1 ounce cold water

Stir Jell-O into cola until powder is completely dissolved. Allow to cool 20 minutes. Add rum and cold water. Mix and pour into shot glasses. Place shots in fridge to set.

A neat set-up shot for this one is easy and fun: arrange groups of 16 shots in triangles, using a rack for a pool game, if you have one. Flip a coin to determine who takes the first shot.

Flying Stag (aka Jägerbomb)

3-ounce package black cherry Jell-O
1 cup Red Bull, brought just to a boil
1 cup chilled Jägermeister

Stir Jell-O into Red Bull until powder is completely dissolved. Allow to cool 20 minutes. Add Jägermeister. Mix and pour into shot glasses. Place shots in fridge to set.

You might not want to play the "Guess what's in it?" game with your guests for this one, unless you're in the mood for an all-nighter.

Mai Tai

3-ounce package pineapple Jell-O
1 cup boiling water
3 ounces chilled light rum
3 ounces chilled dark rum
2 ounces chilled pineapple juice
2 ounces orange juice
2 ounces cranberry juice

Stir Jell-O into boiling water until powder is completely dissolved. Allow to cool 20 minutes. Mix in both rums and all the juice. Pour into shot glasses. Place shots in fridge to set.

Ladyslipper

3-ounce package strawberry Jell-O
1 cup boiling water
7 ounces chilled banana liquor

Stir Jell-O into boiling water until powder is completely dissolved. Allow to cool 20 minutes. Add banana liquor. Mix and pour into shot glasses. Place shots in fridge to set.

Pinguinha

3-ounce package strawberry Jell-O
1 cup boiling water
4 ounces chilled cachaça
¼ cup sugar
cinnamon

Stir Jell-O into boiling water until powder is completely dissolved. Allow to cool 20 minutes. Mix in cachaça and pour into 9" x 12" shallow baking tray. Place tray in fridge to set. When set, cut into cubes and roll in sugar. Add a dash of cinnamon, and this Brazilian treat is ready to go. *Bom proveito!*

Sangria

3-ounce package strawberry Jell-O
1 cup boiling water
½ cup chilled orange juice
1 ounce lemon juice
1½ cups chilled red wine
1 cup total apples, oranges, and
   peaches cut into small pieces
   (try plums, pears, and cherries
   for an alternative)
shaved lime peel (optional)

Stir Jell-O into boiling water until powder is completely dissolved. Allow to cool 20 minutes. Add orange juice, lemon juice, red wine, and mixed fruit. Mix and pour into shot glasses, making sure to even out the fruit between glasses. Place shots in fridge to set. If you'd like, shave a little lime peel onto the top of each glass.

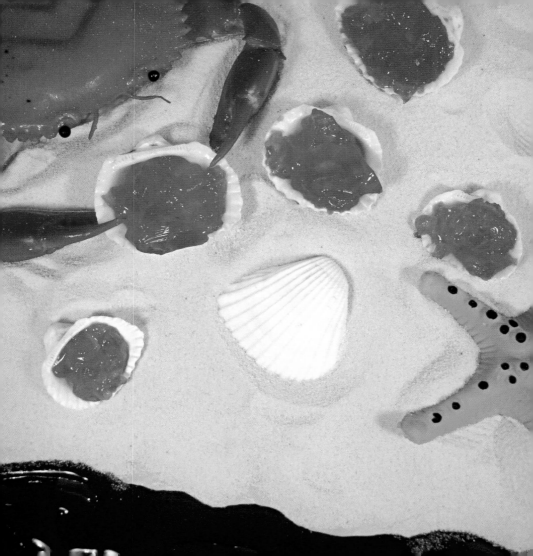

Sex on the Beach

3-ounce package cranberry Jell-O
1 cup orange juice, brought
just to a boil
6 ounces chilled vodka
3 ounces chilled peach schnapps
3 ounces chilled crème de cassis

Stir Jell-O into orange juice until powder is completely dissolved. Allow to cool 20 minutes. Add vodka, peach schnapps, and crème de cassis. Mix and pour into shot glasses. Place shots in fridge to set.

Strawberry Daiquiri

3-ounce package strawberry Jell-O
(or half a package of strawberry
and half a package of lemon)
1 cup boiling water
7 ounces chilled rum
1 ounce lime juice
1 cup sliced fresh strawberries

Stir Jell-O into boiling water until powder is completely dissolved. Allow to cool 20 minutes. Add rum and lime juice. Mix and pour into shot glasses. Place shots in fridge to set. Garnish with fresh strawberries when ready to serve.

Orange

Alabama Cavalier

3-ounce package orange Jell-O
1 cup boiling water
2 ounces chilled Irish whiskey
6 ounces cold water
fresh orange, cut into small pieces

Stir Jell-O into boiling water until powder is completely dissolved. Allow to cool 20 minutes. Add whiskey and cold water. Mix and place in fridge to set. After about an hour, depending on your fridge and how cold the cold liquids were when you added them, fold in the orange pieces and divide the mix into shot glasses and place the shots in the fridge until set. For even more citrus flavor, soak the orange pieces in lemon juice.

Fuzzy Navel

3-ounce package orange Jell-O
1 cup boiling water
2 ounces cold water
6 ounces chilled peach schnapps

Stir Jell-O into boiling water until powder is completely dissolved. Allow to cool 20 minutes. Add cold water and peach schnapps. Mix and pour into shot glasses. Place shots in fridge to set.

Mimosa

3-ounce package orange Jell-O
1 cup champagne, brought
   just to a boil
7 ounces chilled champagne
1 ounce chilled orange juice

Stir Jell-O into boiling champagne until powder is completely dissolved. Allow to cool 20 minutes. Add chilled champagne and orange juice. Mix and pour into shot glasses. Place shots in fridge to set.

Bellini

3-ounce package peach Jell-O
½ cup boiling water
½ cup champagne, brought
   just to a boil
2 ounces chilled champagne
6 ounces chilled vodka

Stir Jell-O into boiling water and heated champagne until powder is completely dissolved. Allow to cool 20 minutes. Add remaining ingredients, mix, and pour into shot glasses. Place shots in fridge to set.

Jell-O shots for brunch! Here are two classic drinks you can eat.

Peach Glacé

3-ounce package peach Jell-O
1 cup boiling water
6 ounces chilled Malibu Rum
2 ounces cold orange juice
2 thinly sliced peaches
5 strawberries (optional)
10 raspberries (optional)

Stir Jell-O into boiling water until powder is completely dissolved. Allow to cool 20 minutes. Add rum and orange juice. Mix and allow to chill for 2 hours. Carefully fold in peaches and divide into shot glasses. Place shots in fridge for another 3 hours to set.

If you like, prepare this shot the old-fashioned way: in a mold, with strawberries or raspberries in the center. Spray the mold with non-stick spray. First make the Jell-O without the fruit, as per the recipe, and place in fridge for 2 hours, then add strawberry or raspberry slices and return to fridge for 4 hours to set. Slice and serve with forks.

Pomegranate Prosecco

3-ounce package apricot Jell-O
¾ cup boiling water
4 ounces chilled PAMA
   Pomegranate Liqueur
6 ounces chilled Prosecco

Stir Jell-O into boiling water until
powder is completely dissolved.
Allow to cool 20 minutes. Add PAMA
Liqueur and Prosecco. Mix and pour
into champagne flutes. Place flutes
in fridge to set.

*For an elegant crowd (read: one that
will take their beverages sitting down),
serve shots with a dainty spoon.*

Three Sheets to the Wind

3-ounce package peach Jell-O
1 cup ginger ale, brought
   just to a boil
8 ounces chilled Captain Morgan
   spiced rum

Stir Jell-O into ginger ale until powder
is completely dissolved. Allow to cool
20 minutes. Add the rum. Mix and pour
into shot glasses. Place shots in fridge
to set but forget level surfaces. These
babies should set on the slant. Find
a way to prop the shots at an angle,
and they'll stay that way. Very cool
effect that is sure to get your guests
buoyed up.

Yellow

Banana Split

3.4-ounce package Jell-O Instant
  Banana Cream Pudding & Pie Filling
¾ cup milk
3 ½ ounces crème de cacao
¾ cup Cool Whip
approximately 40 chocolate chips
maraschino cherries

Mix pudding powder with milk and
allow to sit for a few minutes. Add crème
de cacao and lightly stir in Cool Whip.
Mix in chocolate chips. Scoop into cups,
and put a maraschino cherry on top
of each one. Place cups in fridge until
ready to serve.

*This shot comes out a beautifully pale
yellow. The low alcohol content will make
it just right for those who like a little kick
with their dessert rather than a little
something sweet to go with their spirits.*

Flirtini

3-ounce package pineapple Jell-O
1 cup boiling water
3 ounces chilled vodka
2 ounces chilled champagne
3 ounces chilled Grand Marnier
  orange-flavored liqueur
fresh pineapple, cut into chunks

Stir Jell-O into boiling water until
powder is completely dissolved. Allow
to cool 20 minutes. Add vodka, champagne, and Grand Marnier. Mix and
pour into shot glasses. Place shots
in fridge to set. When ready to serve,
garnish with fresh pineapple. Make
sure you don't try to add pineapple
to the mix: the shot won't set.

Lemon Drop

3-ounce package lemon Jell-O
1 cup boiling water
4 ounces chilled vodka
4 ounces cold water
4 lemons

Delight your guests by serving these shots in lemon slices. Cut lemons in half and remove fruit from the skin (you won't need the fruit itself; you can add to a punch or ice water so it doesn't go to waste).

Stir Jell-O into boiling water until powder is completely dissolved. Allow to cool 20 minutes. Add the vodka and cold water and mix. When the Jell-O is ready, pour into the lemon halves and let chill in fridge. When you're ready to serve, cut the lemon halves into wedges (you'll get roughly 3 from each half). If you like, sprinkle sugar on top.

Lemon Balls

3-ounce package lemon Jell-O
1 cup boiling water
4 ounces chilled bourbon
3 ounces chilled Cointreau
honey

Stir Jell-O into boiling water until powder is completely dissolved. Allow to cool 20 minutes. Add bourbon and Cointreau. Mix and place bowl in fridge to set. Use a melon scoop to make the lemon balls. Arrange them on a platter and drizzle with honey.

Orange Blossom

3.4-ounce package Jell-O Instant
  French Vanilla Pudding & Pie Filling
¾ cup milk
2 ounces Stolichnaya Orange Vodka
2 ounces Triple Sec
1 cup Cool Whip
2–3 graham crackers (optional)

Mix pudding powder with milk and
allow to sit for a few minutes. Add
vodka, Triple Sec, and Cool Whip and
stir until ingredients are blended.
Scoop into cups and place them in
fridge until ready to serve, at which
point you can sprinkle with crushed
graham crackers if you'd like.

Piña Colada

3-ounce package pineapple Jell-O
1 cup boiling water
8 ounces chilled Malibu Rum
fresh pineapple wedges
maraschino cherries

Stir Jell-O into boiling water until
powder is completely dissolved. Allow
to cool 20 minutes. Add rum, mix, and
pour into shot glasses. Place shots
in fridge to set. When you're ready to
serve, garnish with pineapple wedges
and maraschino cherries.

Whiskey in the Jar

1 ounce fresh lemon juice
6 ounces chilled whiskey
2 envelopes unflavored gelatin
  (¼ ounce each)
1 cup lemonade, heated

Mix lemon juice and whiskey, add
gelatin and let sit for a few minutes.
Add heated lemonade, stir, and pour
into jars. Place jars in fridge to set.

Arcadia
3-ounce package lemon Jell-O
1 cup boiling water
5 ounces chilled vodka
3 ounces chilled
  green apple schnapps
10 drops green food coloring

Stir Jell-O into boiling water until
powder is completely dissolved. Allow
to cool 20 minutes. Mix in vodka and
schnapps. Just before you're ready to
pour the shots, add green food coloring. If you want an array of shades from
light green to dark, add a drop or two of
food coloring, mix, and pour into a few
glasses. Next add a few more drops,
mix, and pour into a few more glasses.
Three of each shade makes a nice pre-
sentation. Place shots in fridge to set.
As a variation, try sour apple schnapps.

Apple Mini-tini
3-ounce package lime Jell-O
1 cup apple juice, brought
  just to a boil
5 ounces chilled apple-flavored vodka
3 ounces cold water

Stir Jell-O into apple juice until powder
is completely dissolved. Allow to cool
20 minutes. Add vodka and cold water.
Mix and pour into shot glasses. Place
shots in fridge to set.

Green

Coconut in the Lime

3-ounce package lime Jell-O
6 ounces boiling water
5 ounces chilled coconut rum
2 ounces chilled coconut water

Stir Jell-O into boiling water until powder is completely dissolved. Allow to cool 20 minutes. Add rum and coconut water. Mix and pour into shot glasses. Place shots in fridge to set.

This is a great candidate for using fruit slices to serve the shots. Most likely you don't have coconuts on hand, so try limes instead. Cut fresh limes in wedges and remove fruit from the skin. When the Jell-O mixture is ready, pour into the lime wedges and chill in fridge.

Easy Being Green

3.4-ounce package Jell-O Sugar Free Fat Free Pistachio Pudding Mix
2¼ cups milk
9 ounces light rum
1½ cups Cool Whip

Mix pudding powder with milk and allow to sit for a few minutes. Mix in rum and lightly stir in Cool Whip. Pour into cups and chill until ready to serve.

42

Gin & Tonic
3-ounce package lime Jell-O
½ cup water and ½ cup tonic,
**   combined and brought just to a boil**
6 ounces chilled gin
2 ounces chilled tonic

Stir Jell-O into water and tonic mixture
until the powder is completely dissolved. Allow to cool 20 minutes. Add
chilled gin and tonic. Mix and pour into
shot glasses. Place shots in fridge to set.

*If you'd like, when you're ready to serve,
shave a little lime peel onto the top of
each shot or garnish with a wedge of lime.*

*To get shots that will glow in the dark
(under a black light) use tonic with
quinine in it. Quinine is that bitter-
tasting alkaloid that's used to treat
malaria. Sounds serious, but it's really
just your standard tonic. Who knew
Jell-O shots could be UV reactive?*

Lime Cooler
3-ounce package lime Jell-O
1 cup boiling water
6 ounces chilled Midori melon liqueur
1 ounce sweet and sour mix
1 ounce chilled peach schnapps

Stir Jell-O into boiling water until
powder is completely dissolved.
Allow to cool 20 minutes. Combine
Midori, sweet and sour mix, and peach
schnapps and add to Jell-O. Mix and
pour into shot glasses. Place shots
in fridge to set.

Margaritaville

3-ounce package lime Jell-O
1 cup boiling water
3 ounces chilled tequila
1 ounce chilled Triple Sec
1 ounce chilled lime juice
1 ounce cold water
1 lime, cut in half
margarita salt

Stir Jell-O into boiling water until powder is completely dissolved. Allow to cool 20 minutes. Add tequila, Triple Sec, lime juice, and cold water. Mix and pour into glasses. Place glasses in fridge to set. When you're ready to serve, rub the lime on the edge of the glass and dip in margarita salt. If you have real margarita glasses, be prepared for giant shots. You might even want to serve with a spoon.

If you have only basic supplies on hand, you can mix up a batch of these using just lime Jell-O and tequila. You can also buy margarita-flavored Jell-O seasonally. Try mixing half a margarita-flavored Jell-O package with half a strawberry-flavored package. Prepare according to Margaritaville recipe instructions.

Mojito

3-ounce package lime Jell-O
3-ounce package pineapple Jell-O
1 cup boiling water
1 teaspoon sugar
2 ounces chilled pineapple juice
8 ounces chilled light rum
1 lime

Stir both Jell-O flavors into boiling water until powder is completely dissolved. Add sugar. Whisk together. Allow to cool 20 minutes. Add pineapple juice and rum and squeeze in lime juice. Mix and pour into shot glasses. Place shots in fridge to set.

If you'd like, add fresh mint leaves when you mix in the pineapple juice, rum, and lime juice. Use a mortar and pestle to crush ("bruise" in culinary speak) the leaves so they add their refreshing flavor to the shots.

Blue

Blueberry Cheesecake

3.4-ounce package Jell-O Instant
  Cheesecake Pudding & Pie Filling
1 cup milk
5 ounces blueberry schnapps
1 cup Cool Whip

You'll need cupcake holders to serve up these tasty shots.

Mix pudding powder with milk and allow to sit for a few minutes. Add schnapps and lightly stir in Cool Whip. Scoop into cupcake holders and place in fridge until ready to serve.

Cinco de Mayo

3-ounce package Berry Blue Jell-O
1 cup boiling water
1 cup chilled malt liquor

Stir Jell-O into boiling water until powder is completely dissolved. Allow to cool 20 minutes. Add malt liquor and pour into 7" x 11" baking pan. Place in fridge to set. Cut into triangles to serve.

When you're ready to serve the Cinco de Mayos, place the bottom of the pan in hot water to "release" the Jell-O.

Grenadine Sunset

3-ounce package Berry Blue Jell-O
3-ounce package raspberry Jell-O
1½ cups boiling water
7 ounces chilled Blueberry
   Passion Schnapps
5 ounces vodka
blueberries

Stir both Jell-O flavors into boiling water until powder is completely dissolved. Allow to cool 20 minutes. Add schnapps and vodka. Mix and pour into shot glasses. Place shots in fridge to set. Add one blueberry to each shot as it begins to thicken.

For an eye-catching display, use plastic cups with lids and flip shots over when they've set. When it comes time to serve the shots, remove the cups, and you'll have an array of little blue trapezoids to tempt your visitors.

Kind of Blue

3-ounce package Berry Blue Jell-O
6 ounces boiling water
5 ounces chilled black currant vodka
approximately 20 blueberries

Stir Jell-O into boiling water until powder is completely dissolved. Allow to cool 20 minutes. Add vodka and blueberries, mix together, and pour into shot glasses. Place shots in fridge to set.

Sky-Diving

3-ounce package Berry Blue Jell-O
1 cup 7UP, brought just to a boil
8 ounces chilled DeKuyper Pucker
** Island Blue Schnapps**
whipped cream

Stir Jell-O into 7UP until powder is
completely dissolved. Allow to cool
20 minutes. Add schnapps. Mix and
pour into shot glasses. Add a dollop
of whipped cream to top each shot.
Place in fridge to set.

*Try a muffin pan (sprayed with non-
stick cooking spray) instead of shot
glasses to make cute little blue pools
for your guests to dive into and enjoy.*

Purple

Grape Lake

3-ounce package grape Jell-O
3-ounce package orange Jell-O
1 cup boiling water
2 ounces chilled vodka
2 ounces chilled Triple Sec
2 ounces chilled Chambord

Add a half package of each Jell-O flavor to boiling water and stir until powder is completely dissolved. Allow to cool 20 minutes. Add vodka, Triple Sec, and Chambord and mix. Because of the shot's name, it's fun to serve this one in a shallow dish—preferably a flat, rectangular, or square shape—for that Grape Lake effect. After you've poured the mix into the dish, place in the fridge to set. When ready to serve, cut into squares and stick a toothpick into each one.

Purple Cream (non-alcoholic)

3-ounce package grape Jell-O
½ cup very hot (but not boiling) water
2½ cups cold milk

Stir Jell-O into hot water until powder is completely dissolved. Allow to cool to room temperature. Add cold milk slowly, stirring until the Jell-O and milk are blended. Pour into shot glasses. Place shots in fridge to set.

Purple People Eater

3-ounce package raspberry Jell-O
3-ounce package Berry Blue Jell-O
1½ cups boiling water
8 ounces chilled plum schnapps

Stir both Jell-O flavors into boiling water until powder is completely dissolved. Allow to cool 20 minutes. Add plum schnapps. Mix and pour into shot glasses. Place shots in fridge to set.

Purple Crush

3-ounce package grape Jell-O
8 ounces boiling water
3 ounces chilled amaretto
2 ounces chilled rosé wine
1 ounce chilled vodka

Stir Jell-O into boiling water until powder is completely dissolved. Allow to cool 20 minutes. Add amaretto, wine, and vodka. Mix and place bowl in fridge. Allow to set. To serve, crush up and flake with a fork, dividing into shot glasses. Serve with spoons.

Violet Punch

1 cup chilled grape juice
4 envelopes unflavored gelatin
   (¼ ounce each)
2 cups grape juice,
   brought just to a boil
1 cup Absolut Raspberri Vodka,
   heated

Pour chilled grape juice into bowl and
sprinkle with gelatin. After 15 minutes,
add boiling grape juice and heated
vodka and mix. Place bowl in fridge
to set.

*If you like, serve in a large bowl, as you
would punch. Set out spoons and cups on
the side for guests to serve themselves.*

Pink

Cupid

3-ounce package watermelon Jell-O
1 cup boiling water
6½ ounces chilled Malibu
**   White Rum**
1½ ounces cold water

Stir Jell-O into boiling water until powder is completely dissolved. Allow to cool 20 minutes. Add rum and cold water and mix. Pour into 7" x 11" baking pan and place in fridge to set. Once the mixture has set, use a heart-shaped cookie cutter to cut into servings and then serve on a tray covered with parchment paper. A surefire treat to help make Valentine's Day a success.

*Another Valentine's Day natural is cinnamon schnapps. Try it with strawberry Jell-O.

Fruit Smoothie

6-ounce package Mixed Fruit Jell-O
12 ounces boiling water
8 ounces chilled raspberry vodka
5 ounces chilled whiskey
2 ounces chilled Triple Sec
6 ounces Strawberry & Banana
**   Smoothie** (see below)

Stir Jell-O into boiling water until powder is completely dissolved. Allow to cool 20 minutes. Add remaining ingredients. Mix and pour into shot glasses. Place shots in fridge to set.

Strawberry & Banana Smoothie

½ frozen banana
3 large strawberries
1 tablespoon plain yogurt
4 ounces orange juice

In a blender, mix ingredients together.

Mondays

**3-ounce package Strawberry-
   Kiwi Jell-O
1 cup boiling water
5½ ounces chilled
   Bacardi Limón rum
2½ ounces cold water**

Stir Jell-O into boiling water until
powder is completely dissolved. Allow
to cool 20 minutes. Add remaining
ingredients. Mix and pour into 7" x 11"
baking pan. Place pan in fridge to set.
When mix has set and you're ready to
serve the concoction, make fun shapes
with cookie cutters and chase away
those Monday Blues.

Nantucket

**3-ounce package cranberry Jell-O
1 cup grapefruit juice, brought
   to just a boil
5 ounces chilled brandy
3 ounces cold water**

Stir Jell-O into grapefruit juice until
powder is completely dissolved. Allow
to cool 20 minutes. Add brandy and
water. Mix and pour into shot glasses.
Place shots in fridge to set.

Raspberry Cheesecake

4-ounce package Jell-O Instant Cheesecake Pudding & Pie Filling
¾ cup milk
3 ounces raspberry schnapps
2 ounces light rum
8 ounces Cool Whip
3 graham crackers

Mix pudding into milk and allow to sit for a few minutes. Mix in raspberry schnapps and rum. Lightly stir in Cool Whip. Pour into cups and chill until ready to serve. Before serving, sprinkle crushed graham crackers on top.

This shot gets a lot of comparisons to Laffy Taffy candy. If you're feeling inspired, write a silly joke on the bottom of each cup. Use paper cups or plastic cups with labels on the bottom.

Waikiki

3-ounce package cherry Jell-O
1 cup 7UP, brought to just a boil
3 ounces chilled orange juice
5 ounces chilled gin
maraschino cherries

Stir Jell-O into 7UP until powder is completely dissolved. Allow to cool 20 minutes. Add orange juice and gin. Mix and pour into shot glasses. Place shots in fridge to set.

Maraschino cherries are de rigueur. Put one on top of each shot, but make sure to wait until the mixture has begun to thicken up enough so the cherry won't sink down to the bottom of the glass.

Some say the Shirley Temple——the famous cocktail for kids——was invented at a hotel in Waikiki; others give credit for the famous "Grenadine Lemonade" to Chasen's in Hollywood. Either way, save this version for the over-21 crowd.

Watermelon Elixir

6-ounce package watermelon Jell-O
1½ cups boiling water
1 pint watermelon sherbet
1 ounce lemon juice
3 ounces chilled vodka

In a large bowl, stir Jell-O into boiling water until powder is completely dissolved. Allow to cool 20 minutes. Add sherbet, lemon juice, and vodka and mix. Pour into martini glasses and chill until set.

For an extra flavor kick, try this with watermelon-infused vodka.

Black

Jack of Hearts

3-ounce package black cherry Jell-O
1 cup boiling water
5 ounces chilled vanilla vodka
3 drops blue food coloring
3 drops red food coloring
2 ounces cold water
whipped cream

Stir Jell-O into boiling water until powder is completely dissolved. Allow to cool 20 minutes. Add vodka, food coloring, and cold water. Mix and pour into shot glasses. Place shots in fridge to set. Serve each with a dollop of whipped cream.

Straight Nines

6-ounce package black cherry Jell-O
1½ cups boiling water
8 ounces chilled amaretto
3 drops blue food coloring (optional)
3 drops red food coloring (optional)

Stir Jell-O into boiling water until powder is completely dissolved. Allow to cool 20 minutes. Add amaretto and blend. If you like, add a few drops of blue and red food coloring to make the shot look black. Mix and pour into shot injectors for an extra-creepy treat. This will make twice as much as the standard recipe. Chill as usual.

Midnight Rambler

½ 3-ounce package grape Jell-O
½ 3-ounce package orange Jell-O
1 cup boiling water
4 ounces chilled vodka
3 ounces crème de cassis
1 ounce cold water

Stir Jell-O into boiling water until powder is completely dissolved. Allow to cool 20 minutes. Add vodka, crème de cassis, and cold water. Mix and pour into shot glasses. Place shots in fridge to set.

B-52

3.3-ounce package Jell-O Instant
   White Chocolate Pudding &
   Pie Filling
1 cup cold milk
3 ounces Kahlúa
2 ounces amaretto
1 ounce Irish Cream

Mix pudding powder with milk and
allow to sit for a few minutes. Add
rest of ingredients and mix. Pour into
shot glasses. These are ready to serve!
Remind your guests these are traditional shots (as in, you drink them neat)
rather than edible cocktails.

Brown

Brandy Cream

**3.4-ounce package Jell-O Instant
  Vanilla Pudding & Pie Filling**
1 cup cold milk
4 ounces brandy
2 ounces crème de cacao

Mix pudding powder with milk and
allow to sit for a few minutes. Add
brandy and crème de cacao and mix.
Pour into shot glasses. These are ready
to serve! Remind your guests these are
traditional shots (as in, you drink them
neat) rather than edible cocktails.

Chocolate-Lemon Cooler

**3.4-ounce package Jell-O Instant
  Lemon Pudding & Pie Filling**
**½ ounce Jell-O Instant Chocolate
  Pudding & Pie Filling**
1¼ cups milk
6 ounces Captain Morgan spiced rum
1 cup Cool Whip

Mix lemon pudding powder and chocolate pudding powder with milk and allow
to sit for a few minutes. Add rum and
lightly stir in Cool Whip. Scoop into cups
and keep in fridge until ready to serve.

The Hustler

3.4-ounce package Jell-O Instant
  Pumpkin Pudding & Pie Filling
¾ cup cold milk
6 ounces caramel liquor
1 cup Cool Whip
whipped cream
nutmeg

Mix pudding powder with milk and allow to sit for a few minutes. Add liquor and lightly stir in Cool Whip. Scoop into cups, top each with a dollop of whipped cream, and sprinkle with nutmeg. Chill until ready to serve.

Pumpkin flavor is seasonal——watch for it in early fall.

Irish Pudding

3.9-ounce package Jell-O Instant
  Chocolate Pudding & Pie Filling
¾ cup cold milk
2 ounces vodka
4 ounces Irish cream
1 cup Cool Whip
2 bananas, cut into small pieces
whipped cream
cinnamon

Mix pudding powder with milk and allow to sit for a few minutes. Add vodka, Irish cream, and mix. Lightly stir in Cool Whip. Mix in bananas and scoop into cups. Add a dollop of whipped cream to each shot and sprinkle with cinnamon. These are ready to serve. Enjoy!

Malibu Lagoon

**3.9-ounce package Jell-O Instant
  Chocolate Pudding & Pie Filling**
1 cup cold milk
5 ounces Malibu Coconut Rum
1 cup Cool Whip

Mix pudding powder with milk and
allow to sit for a few minutes. Add rum
and lightly stir in Cool Whip. Pour into
cups and freeze.

Mousse Pops

**3.8-ounce package Jell-O Instant
  Devil's Food Pudding & Pie Filling**
¾ cup milk
2 ounces vodka
4 ounces Irish cream
8 ounces Cool Whip

You'll need popsicle molds for this.

Mix pudding powder with milk and
allow to sit for a few minutes. Mix in
vodka and Irish cream. Lightly stir
in Cool Whip. Pour into popsicle molds
and chill until ready to serve.

White Russian Pony

**3.9-ounce package Jell-O Instant
 Chocolate Pudding & Pie Filling
¾ cup cold milk
4 ounces Kahlúa
2 ounces Irish cream
1 ounce vodka
1 cup Cool Whip**

Mix pudding powder with milk and
allow to sit for a few minutes. Mix in
Kahlúa, Irish cream, and vodka.
Lightly stir in Cool Whip. Pour into
cups and freeze.

Oompa-Loompa

**½ cup cold water
½ cup cold milk
2 envelopes unflavored gelatin
 (¼ ounce each)
2 tablespoons smooth peanut butter
 (not an all-natural brand)
½ cup amaretto
chocolate syrup**

Mix water and milk and sprinkle
with gelatin powder. Allow to sit for
15 minutes. Mix in peanut butter,
amaretto, and a few squirts of
chocolate syrup. Pour into cups and
place in fridge until ready to serve.

White

Coconut Dream

3.4-ounce package Jell-O Instant
   Coconut Cream Pudding &
   Pie Filling
¾ cup milk
6 ounces Absolut Mango Vodka
1 cup Cool Whip

Mix pudding powder with milk and allow to sit for a few minutes. Add vodka and mix. Lightly stir in Cool Whip. Scoop into cups and place in fridge until ready to serve.

To enhance the tropical mood, top each shot with a sprinkle of shaved coconut when ready to serve.

Cookies 'n Cream Pie

4.2-ounce package Jell-O Instant
   Oreo Cookies 'n Cream Pudding
   & Pie Filling
¾ cup milk
2 ounces Kahlúa
2 ounces vanilla vodka
1 cup Cool Whip, plus extra
   for layering
graham cracker or any premade
   crust, prepared according to
   instructions

Mix pudding powder with milk and allow to sit for a few minutes. Add Kahlúa and vodka, then lightly stir in Cool Whip. Scoop into crust, cover with a thin layer of Cool Whip and place in fridge until ready to serve.

This is an honest-to-very-goodness pie, not a shot, but you can serve slices in martini glasses or brandy snifters or any barware that will support the crust. Don't forget to provide guests with spoons.

Sienna Slammer

**3.4-ounce package Jell-O Instant
  Vanilla Pudding & Pie Filling
¾ cup eggnog
4 ounces Grand Marnier
  orange-flavored liqueur
1 cup Cool Whip**

Mix pudding powder with eggnog and
allow to sit for a few minutes. Add Grand
Marnier and lightly stir in Cool Whip.
Scoop into cups and place in fridge until
ready to serve.

Winter Solstice

**3.3-ounce package Jell-O Instant
  White Chocolate Pudding &
  Pie Filling
¾ cup milk
4 ounces vanilla vodka
1 cup Cool Whip
fresh strawberries, sliced**

Mix pudding powder with milk and allow
to sit for a few minutes. Mix in vodka.
Lightly stir in Cool Whip. Scoop into
cups, add one strawberry slice to the
top of each, and place in fridge until
ready to serve.

Tea Time

4 ounces cold green tea
2 envelopes unflavored gelatin
  (¼ ounce each)
6 ounces green tea,
  brought to just a boil
¼ cup sugar
pinch salt
6 ounces heated green tea liqueur

Pour cold tea into 9" x 12" shallow baking pan. Sprinkle gelatin powder over tea. Let sit for 15 minutes. Add hot tea, sugar, and salt and stir. Add heated green tea liqueur, mix, and place in fridge to set. When ready to serve, cut into cubes.

Up your antioxidants as you enjoy this refreshing green-tea treat! To round out the tea ceremony, pair with biscotti and sliced kumquats.

Clear

Gummy Suspension

1 cup cold water
2 envelopes unflavored gelatin
  (¼ ounce each)
1 cup grain alcohol, heated to warm
gummy candies

Sprinkle cold water with gelatin. Allow to sit for a few minutes. Add grain alcohol, mix, and put bowl in fridge. After 15 minutes, remove bowl, and scoop out tablespoon-size shots with one hand, add a gummy to each spoonful with the other, and fill individual shot glasses, one gummy to each. Add more Jell-O on top of the candy if needed to get it as close to the middle of the shot as possible.

Use clear plastic or glass cups, since the whole point is to be able to see the gummy. If you use gummy worms, have part of each wriggling out from a shot. You can suspend a gummy bear fully in a shot.

For more fun, mix gummies, with worms dangling from the top and bears floating in the shot.

For giant gummies that will make your guests think they are seeing things, soak the candies overnight in vodka, and then follow the rest of the shot recipe.

Bait 'n' Switch

First Layer: Orange
3-ounce package peach Jell-O
1 cup boiling water
6 ounces chilled peach vodka
2 ounces cold water

Second Layer: Blue
3-ounce package Berry Blue Jell-O
1 cup boiling water
6 ounces chilled blueberry vodka
2 ounces cold water

First Layer: Stir peach Jell-O into boiling water until powder is completely dissolved. Allow to cool 20 minutes. Add vodka and water. Pour into shot glasses, allowing room for the second layer, and place in fridge for at least 30 minutes.

Second Layer: Repeat first layer's steps, and return shot glasses to fridge to fully set.

Try to remember "what's in these," when your guests start asking questions!

Rainbow

The trick to layered Jell-O shots is to allow each layer to half set: When you wiggle the cup, the shot shakes, but it doesn't slosh. This takes about 30 minutes to an hour. Then, you can add the shot's next layer.

Since part of the fun of these shots is the assortment of colors, you'll definitely want to serve them in clear glasses or cups. You can prepare them as stand-alone jigglers, too. To make jigglers, chill shot mix in a 7" x 11" baking pan and then cut into squares or, using cookie cutters, cut into shapes.

Cheesecake Combo

For this one, make one batch of the recipe with raspberry schnapps and one with vanilla schnapps—fill the glasses half and half. For an even more eye-catching display, alternate which flavor goes on top.

First Layer: 3.4-ounce package Jell-O Instant Cheesecake Pudding & Pie Filling
¾ cup milk
5 ounces raspberry schnapps
8 ounces Cool Whip

Mix pudding powder with milk and allow to sit for a few minutes. Mix in raspberry schnapps. Lightly stir in Cool Whip. Pour layer into glasses and place in fridge while you make the next layer.

Second Layer: 3.4-ounce package Jell-O Instant Cheesecake Pudding & Pie Filling
¾ cup milk
5 ounces vanilla schnapps
8 ounces Cool Whip
crushed graham crackers (used to top shots after both layers are in glasses)

Mix pudding powder with milk and allow to sit for a few minutes. Mix in vanilla schnapps. Lightly stir in Cool Whip. Bring first-layer cups out of fridge, and gently scoop a layer of vanilla pudding on top of each one. When you're ready to serve, sprinkle crushed graham crackers on top of each shot.

Chocolate Raspberry Parfait

First Layer: 3-ounce package raspberry Jell-O
1 cup boiling water
6 ounces chilled Smirnoff Black Cherry Vodka

Stir Jell-O into boiling water until powder is completely dissolved. Allow to cool about 20 minutes. Add vodka, mix, pour into shot glasses (leaving enough room for the second layer), and place glasses in fridge until set.

Second Layer: 3.9-ounce package Jell-O Chocolate Instant Pudding & Pie Filling
¾ cup milk
4 ounces espresso vodka
1 cup Cool Whip

Mix pudding powder with milk and allow to sit for a few minutes. Add vodka, and then lightly stir in Cool Whip. Keep in fridge until ready to use. When the Jell-O layer has set, add a layer of pudding mix to each shot.

Holly Jolly Christmas

First Layer: Red
½ package cranberry Jell-O
   (1½ ounces)
½ package raspberry Jell-O
   (1½ ounces)
1 cup boiling water
4 ounces chilled cinnamon schnapps
4 ounces vodka

Second Layer: Green
3-ounce package lime Jell-O
1 cup boiling water
5 ounces chilled vodka

First Layer: Stir both Jell-O flavors into boiling water until powder is completely dissolved. Allow to cool 20 minutes. Add cinnamon schnapps and vodka and mix. Pour into shot glasses (don't fill more than halfway, to save room for the other layer) and place in fridge for at least 30 minutes.

Second Layer: Stir Jell-O into boiling water until powder is completely dissolved. Allow to cool 20 minutes. Add vodka and mix. Pour over first layer and place shot glasses back into fridge to set. When ready to serve, arrange glasses in the shape of a Christmas tree.

Twilight's Last Gleaming

First Layer: Red
3-ounce package cherry Jell-O
6 ounces boiling water
5 ounces chilled light rum
15 cut-up pitted cherries

Second Layer: White
2 envelopes unflavored gelatin
(¼ ounce each)
2 ounces cold water
¾ cup coconut milk
½ cup sugar
1 teaspoon vanilla extract
½ cup whipped cream

Third Layer: Blue
3-ounce package Berry Blue Jell-O
6 ounces boiling water
5 ounces chilled blueberry vodka
3 ounces cold water
30 blueberries

First layer: Stir cherry Jell-O into boiling water until powder is completely dissolved. Allow to cool 20 minutes. Add rum and gently stir in cherries. Pour into a baking pan and place in fridge for at least 20 minutes.

Second layer: Mix gelatin and cold water. Heat coconut milk in a saucepan and mix in sugar. Bring to a boil (keep stirring). Add to gelatin mixture, along with vanilla extract. Mix ingredients well and cool for 15 minutes. Stir in the whipped cream and spread over red layer and return baking pan to fridge for another 20 minutes.

Third layer: Stir Berry Blue Jell-O into boiling water until completely dissolved. Allow to cool 20 minutes. Add vodka, cold water, and blueberries. Spoon over the white layer and return baking pan to fridge. When set, cut into cubes or—even better—use a cookie cutter to make stars!

Volume Equivalents

These are not exact equivalents for American cups and spoons,
but have been rounded up or down slightly to make measuring easier.

American	Metric	Fluid Ounces
2 tbsp	30 ml	1 fl oz
3 tbsp	45 ml	1 1/2 fl oz
1/4 cup (4 tbsp)	60 ml	2 fl oz
1/3 cup (5 tbsp)	75 ml	2 1/2 fl oz
3/8 cup (6 tbsp)	90 ml	3 fl oz
1/2 cup (8 tbsp)	120 ml	4 fl oz
5/8 cup (10 tbsp)	150 ml	5 fl oz
2/3 cup (11 tbsp)	165 ml	5 1/2 fl oz
3/4 cup (12 tbsp)	180 ml	6 fl oz
7/8 cup (14 tbsp)	210 ml	7 fl oz
1 cup (16 tbsp)	240 ml	8 fl oz
1 1/4 cups	300 ml	10 fl oz

Weight Equivalents

American	Metric
1/4 oz	10 g
1/2 oz	15 g
2/3 oz	20 g
3/4 oz	25 g
1 oz	30 g
1 1/4 oz	35 g
1 1/2 oz	40 g
1 3/4 oz	50 g
2 oz	55 g
2 1/4 oz	65 g
2 1/2 oz	70 g
2 3/4 oz	75 g
3 oz	85 g
3 1/4 oz	90 g
3 1/2 oz	100 g

Soundtracks

"Banana Pudding" Southern Culture on the Skids

"Chocolate Pudding" Mighty Mighty Bosstones

"Gettin' Jiggy wit It" Will Smith

"Jelly Jungle of Orange Marmalade" The Lemon Pipers

"Parade of the Jelly Babies" The Gollywogs

"Peaches and Cream" Beck

"Pour Some Sugar on Me" Def Leppard

"Pudding Time" Primus

"Purple People Eater" Sheb Wooley

"Shake It Up" The Cars

"Shake, Rattle, and Roll" Bill Haley

"Strawberry Cream Puff" Shonen Knife

"We Wish You a Merry Christmas"
(Was anyone before or since so charmingly insistent
on figgy pudding as these carolers?)